Mira Fischer

So I won't get lost
in the dark

Poems

Autorin: Mira Fischer
Umschlagfoto: Mira Fischer
Umschlaggestaltung: Lotte Hauss

Verlag & Druck: tredition GmbH, Halenreie 40-44, 22359 Hamburg
ISBN Taschenbuch: 978-3-347-27683-3
ISBN Hardcover: 978-3-347-27684-0
ISBN e-Book: 978-3-347-27685-7

Bibliografische Information der Deutschen Nationalbibliothek:
Die Deutsche Nationalbibliothek verzeichnet diese Publikation in der
Deutschen Nationalbibliografie; detaillierte bibliografische Daten sind
im Internet über http://dnb.d-nb.de abrufbar.

PRELUDE

Only few words

My soul knows
only few words
soil – tree – sun – bird – sky
simple words, frank and open
like a child's face
or the palm of your hand
or a glass of water on the window sill.

Each word one syllable –
so short they can easily be overlooked
and neglected.

Decent people keep them
in the lowest drawer of their cupboard
and forget.
They are excited about other words:
result, agenda, argument.

But my soul feels bored and lonely in their company
and keeps returning
to the simple words
looks at them closely
and sometimes catches a glimpse
of a former hidden feature –
a new wrinkle in a familiar face.

WAITING IN THE DARK

The lover I return to

Sometimes
something is tugging at my body
from the inside
something that feels
trapped and restless.
It wonders:
Why spend this life in a cage
when you can roam the skies freely
like a bird that knows
its home is somewhere else?
And a flock of geese
is pecking at my skin
with beaks always angry,
always hungry – and never satisfied.

And I cannot bear
even the hands of a lover.

And the only lover
I return to
hides out in the place
where poetry arises.

And even a friend's voice
is a disturbance
and even a warm conversation
will chase away this lover
who is shy and cautious
like a deer
ready to leap into the dark
if I make a sudden move.

This lover does not show up in public
he despises the crowd
and he is a master of sneaking away unnoticed.
But he is waiting, patiently
in the shade of the woods
where the grass grows high
and the animals that cannot be tamed
take refuge.

And for sure he'll still be there
when I turn my gaze away from the lights
and sit quietly and look out
for his eyes in the dark, shining.

And when there's nothing else to hold onto
I will fall back into his arms.

Deeper Currents

You don't have to understand
every little pattern the water draws
in the ocean that you call your life.

Sometimes you just hear
the constant roaring of the sea
and you miss her fine voice.

Sometimes you stay in the shallow waters,
you watch the waves hit the rock – and retreat.
Or your attention is drawn by strange whirls,
stones thrown into quiet waters.

I know you get angry and irritated
by the disturbance they cause.
But what if you take a step back,
what if you allow the waters
to flow in their own pace and direction?

Know this: There are different currents in your life.

What you need is trust, dear,
trust in the wisdom of the sea,
trust in something that is moving
beneath the surface,
in the deeper waters, the darker places,
out of sight and reach.

I know you're a little pretentious
thinking you have grasped it all.
But the sea is not there for you

to fill her in a glass jar and stare at it
waiting for the answers
to pour out.

Rather – the sea will keep her secrets to herself
until you are quiet
until you take a step back
and let the deeper currents emerge.

CONVERSATIONS WITH A BELOVED

Two Kinds of Beauty

You have so many beautiful words
like a bunch of flowers
and with your generous heart
you are giving them away freely.

I might not have as many beautiful words
as you do
but I have music and silence
and in silence I sit down and listen
to the golden stream inside.

Let us invite those silent
but nourishing waves of life
to water the new seed
so it may grow and blossom
and finally reveal
its wondrous beauty.

Violin Strings

Violin strings
caught your ears and your eyes
were caught by fingers
playing the strings.

It was not the voice of the siren you heard
but the sound worked its magic anyway.
And what the strings did not tell you –
your imagination had no trouble
filling the gap.

Now you turned me
into a violin string
tense in expectation
of magical fingers and beautiful melodies
that my imagination has heard long ago.

But also tense in fear of
what heedless fingers may cause:
false notes, discords, screeching, tears.

And one thought troubles me:
What if the tension gets too strong?
Will the string bear it –
or will it tear?

Candle and Firework

If you're the firework,
I am the candle.
When you blow up
it's a marvellous racket.
But if you don't blow me out
I can burn for hours.

This is how you won me over

You take everything life offers you
without a second glance or thought.
There is no option of withdrawal
but only the moment of biting,
may it be an opportunity, a promise
or my left foot.

And when you get hold of it
you will not let go –
of your prey or a dream
or my leg, squeezed tightly
between your knees.

If he is running,
no one can stop
the king of the prairie.

But when you're sleeping
your slim body might still be ready
to jump any minute
but the soles of your feet
call for protection.

Don't buy me a fancy dress

Don't buy me a fancy dress,
just knit me a sweater for cold days
when the fog is as thick as milk powder
and lingers on like a bad dream.

Don't worry about the materials.
I don't need fine silk – wool will do the job.
But if you can, please look for a strong fibre
that won't tear easily.
I like it soft like a baby's cheek
or a chestnut: warm and round and shining
in your hand.

You ask about the colours? – I'm not picky.
But choose a design
that makes me stand out in the crowd
so you'll spot me in an instant.
And maybe you can attach some reflectors
so I won't get lost in the dark.

Don't be concerned about the size.
I'll be happy to wear a loose-fitting garment
with overlong sleeves –
as long as it isn't itchy around the neck.

And don't get disheartened,
if you make a mistake.
I don't mind loose stitches.
If the wind blows harshly,
your fingers may cover the holes.

Instead of "I love you"

Instead of "I love you" I say:
Something in me could love
Something in you
Something in me trusts
Something in you.
And when we find ourselves
behind a locked door
or in a deep ditch
or faced with a road block:
All cards stacked against us and everything at stake –
Something in me will reach out for
Something in you
Something in me will take
Something in you
by the hand
and hold onto it.

A LOOK AT THE SKY

Three Eyes

Cycling home at dusk
my eyes turn up to the sky
and spot what they seek:
Three stars in one perfect line,
the vast blue sky looking down
with three shining eyes.

In this moment I know
my two small eyes can rest for a while
I close them and fall gladly
into the dark space that comes
after the sharp light of the day
that lets shadows grow tall
and thoughts turn stale.
I shake them off like dead skin or feathers
I only needed to get through that day.

Fresh and naked
I await the night.

When I Looked up at the Sky tonight

When I looked up at the sky tonight
I saw the red moon, bright and dusty.
She wore a gray coat like my feet down here
that carry this body so lightly.

Tonight I also met someone new,
her name was Mira, like mine.
Though we share much more
than this little word –
a feeling of being home.

"Your anger grew less
with this world down here",
were the words that I heard tonight.
And I realized to my own surprise:
Some clouds disappear like the evening's light
that leaves nothing but warmth behind.

BODY AS HOME

My Body Keeps Whispering

My mind is a racer:
keeps running and jumping
for an aim in the distance,
always stretching and grabbing
for a flickering image.

My body keeps whispering:
Slow down, dear,
Right here, dear.

My mind is a spider:
It crawls and bends
in the strangest positions,
it climbs up the wall
to look down from the ceiling.

My body keeps whispering:
Down here, dear,
Right here, dear.

My mind is an actor,
an expert at playing,
switches voice and appearance,
knows the tricks of delusion.

My body keeps whispering:
Be true, dear,
Right here, dear.

My mind is a stranger
who has lost his origin,

he fled from a prison
that was built by himself.

My body keeps whispering:
Calm down, dear,
Come home, here.

Dancer on the Subway

I step on the subway
and I spot someone moving
at the opposite door.
A teenager swinging
along to his music – I think –
but then a fire lights up
and I see something different:
The fluidity of your body,
the light in your smile.

And I can't look away
but you don't see me anyway.
Your attention is turned somewhere else,
to this secret well of pleasure
streaming from the plugs in your ears
into your body and out,
revealing itself
in your otherworldly smile.

I see the beauty of opposites right there:
you're a Buddha of detachment
and at the same time present,
in love with your body
which gives you so much delight
with its smoothness, fluid light.
But the gestures of your hands
are exact and precise,
your choreography carefully chosen
from the wide range
of possible movements.

I see in your mind
the perfect performance
you will give on the stage —
this moment is just
a glimpse of a coming joy.

I wish you could show me
how to be at home in my body
and to teach me
how my poetry can be
like this dance
joyful and smooth and at ease
with itself, flowing freely
like a stream of pure light
self-aware but oblivious
to an onlooker's stare.

INVITATIONS

Patient old Guests

You cannot be safe in this world
even your little room,
four walls and a roof
don't make a shelter.

What if you opened the window
to the darkening light?

Don't you see the trees
swaying in the wind
like patient old guests?
They are swinging
to the same music
that set them in motion
long ago.

Don't you hear the rain
patting the roof
like a tireless drummer?
It won't stop playing
it's familiar tune
as long as there are guests,
dancing.

Fall is here.
We are moving into the dark again.
When the night falls
There is a sweetness and tenderness in the woods,
Drawing us closer.

***

My home is
The wind in the trees
The whirling leaves
And the clouds travelling fast in the sky.

My prayer is
The light breaking through the clouds
The chirping of the birds in October
The darkness of the woods at night.

***

The half moon in the black sky
Reminds me of growing space
Between things in winter.
And walking this path I feel
The trees on each side
Are inviting me
To move forward into the caressing darkness
Waiting to take me into her embrace.

What if

What if
for a moment
you could deepen your compassion
to include yourself as part of the whole?

What if
for the span of a breath
you could make peace with yourself
even the ugly and helpless parts
that feel abandoned and broken?

What if
– right now –
you could spread your wings and fly high –
the happiest bird in the sky?

What if
in this very instant
you could stop wandering
realising you have already reached
your destination?

You could stop searching
knowing you have found
the right place at the right time
and you have brought
just the gift that is needed.

Your friends around the table say:
Welcome.
Take a seat.
We are glad you are here.

Special Guest

All week I'm waiting
for Saturday night.
Appointments are cancelled,
phone calls postponed –
I'm expecting a special guest.

In the evening I prepare the dinner.
Walking back and forth
from the stove to the table
does not feel like doing chores
but like a joyful dance
carrying purpose in itself.

There is a perfect silence –
and then time settles back on my sofa
relaxes its muscles
stretches its arms and legs
and lets out a big yawn –
finally it can rest.

FAREWELL

The Sun is in Love

Did you know
that the sun is in love
with the rooftops, the chimneys, the church tower?
It likes to linger at the top floor
spilling its golden light generously
over plastered white walls and smooth yellow bricks
caressing the edges
with its red tongue,
setting them on fire –
What a passionate lover!
What a glorious farewell!

Deep gratitude to:
Lotte Hauss, for the cover art and her aesthetic sensitivity,
Elske Tiller-Thaden, for her encouragement and friendship,
Angela Fischer, for her creative suggestions and support.

Mira Fischer,
born in 1988 in Germany,
writer, poet, editor, dreamer.

Mira Fischer,
1988 in Deutschland geboren,
Autorin, Dichterin, Lektorin, Traumtänzerin.

Zeitfracht Medien GmbH
Ferdinand-Jühlke-Straße 7
99095 Erfurt, Deutschland
produktsicherheit@kolibri360.de